100 Chutney Varieties

By

Mrs.S.Mallika Badrinath   B.Sc (Home Science)

"Cooking Made Easier"
"Wishful cooking made a reality"
with Books on Cookery & M.H.P Masala powders
by Mrs.S.Mallika Badrinath

<u>**Publishers & Books Sellers:**</u>
PRADEEP ENTERPRISES
No:20 (Old No:90), Poes Garden,
Chennai: 600 086. India.
Phone : 44-24990872 / 24997130
email: mhpmasala@gmail.com

Price: Rs. 50/-

First Edition: June 2004
Fifth Reprint: May 2013
@ Copy rights reserved
Photos by R.Ramanidharan

Our books on cookery:

In English:

In Telugu:

In Hindi

Printed at:
Chennai Micro Print, Chennai:29

In Tamil:

In Kannada:

MHP
Masala

**For Quality & Taste Use MHP Masala Produsts By
Culinary Expert & TV Fame *Mrs.S.Mallika Badrinath*
Available with Nilgiris, Fresh & Other Dept Stores**

PREFACE

Generally our South Indian Breakfast consists mainly Idli, dosa, pongal, uppuma varieties. Normally very few chutney varieties are prepared as side dish for these tiffin varieties.

In this book different tasty chutney recipes have been compiled. In many recipes vegetables are used to make it nutritious as well as tasty.

For differnt tiffen item, we have given a suitable chutney suggestion chart. Like my other cook books, this book also will be useful in everyday cooking to make it tasty.

Chennai - 86
Date : 20-7-2004

Mrs. S. Mallika Badrinath

CONTENTS

SUGGESTED CHUTNEY FOR DIFFERENT TIFFIN VARIETIES

Name of the Tiffen	Chutney - Recipe Numbers
Idli Varieties	1-8, 12, 15-30, 36, 39-48, 50, 54-58, 60, 61-87, 89, 90, 100
Dosai Varieties	1-19, 22-26, 28, 30, 36-50, 54-58, 60-90, 97, 99
Pongal, Uppuma Varieties	1, 4, 5, 7, 15, 38, 42, 48, 52, 54, 69, 70, 72, 81, 82, 83-89, 91-94
Bonda, Bajji, Vadai Varieties	1, 4-7, 34, 41-44, 45, 52, 54, 56, 81, 82, 96
Kachori, Samosa Varieties	15, 23, 29, 34, 95, 96, 98, 99, 100
Pani puri, Bhel puri	17, 35, 39, 98
Bread Sandwich	20, 27, 29, 31, 37, 38, 45, 46-47, 49, 54, 60-64, 69, 70, 74, 81, 82, 90, 96, 100
Paniyaram Varieties	1, 4, 5-7, 9-11, 42-44, 48, 50, 56-59, 61, 72, 77, 81, 82
Cutlet Varieties	15, 19, 21, 27, 29, 31-34, 96, 98
Adai Varieties	1, 4-7, 9-14, 23, 26, 27, 30, 36-42, 48-50, 54, 56-59, 63, 68-70, 71-79, 81, 82, 87, 90
Puri, Chappathi Varieties	23, 24, 26, 38, 42, 48, 50, 53, 54-61, 64, 68-70, 73-82, 85, 96, 97, 99, 100

Coconut Chutney Varieties

1. Coconut Chutney

Ingredients:

Grated fresh Coconut - ½ Cup
Roasted gram - ½ cup
Green chillies - 5
Tamarind - Small gooseberry sized
Salt - ¾ tsp.
Asafoetida - little
Oil - 1 tsp.
Mustard - ¼ tsp.
Curry leaves - 2 springs
Red chilli - 1 (broken)

Method:

1. Soak tamarind in little water for 10 minutes.

2. Put coconut, chilli, Roasted gram, tamarind, salt, asafoetida in a mixie and run at low speed once without adding water.

3. Pour just enough water in it and grind to a coarse paste.

4. Heat one teaspoon of oil, add mustard allow to splutter and mix curry leaves, broken chilli in that hot oil. Pour over chutney.

5. Mix well and serve with Idli or dosa varieties.

Variation:

1. Add ½ bunch of coriander leaves and grind chutney.

2. ½ inch piece of ginger can be added along with other ingredients. Ginger and coriander both can be added.

3. **Red Chilli Chutney:** Add more chillies. Reduce quantity of coconut and add roasted gram. Use red chillies instead of green chillies.

4. Add few peeled small onions also while using red chillies for grinding chutney, which adds taste to chutney.

5. **Coconut sweet Chutney:** Omit roasted gram. Grind grated coconut with green chillies, salt, jaggery, asafoetida and little tamarind extract. Serve as a sweet, spicy chutney along with Idlis.

2. Coconut Lemon Chutney

Ingredients:

Grated fresh Coconut - ¾ cup
Green chillies - 3
Cumin seeds - ½ tsp.
Salt - ½ tsp.
Lemon - 1 (small)

Seasoning:

Oil - 1 tsp.
Mustard seeds - ¼ tsp.
Curry leaves - 2 springs

Method:

1. Grind coconut, green chillies, cumin and salt together, with little water to a coarse paste.

2. Squeeze lemon and mix the juice with chutney.

3. Heat oil and season mustard and curry leaves in it. Pour over chutney.

4. Serve with Idli or dosa varieties.

Banana Stem Chutney:

1. Reduce coconut in the above recipe. Chop raw banana stem finely and steam cook it. Grind it along with other ingredients as chutney.

   [Those who want to reduce coconut in their diet can prepare chutney like this which is very healthy and low in calorie.]

1 Table spoon = 3 teaspoons

3. Tofu Chutney (Soya Paneer Chutney)

Ingredients:

Graded fresh Coconut - 3 Tbl.sps.
Green chillies - 5
Ginger - ½ inch piece
Salt - ½ tsp.
Grated Tofu - 2 Tbl.sps.
Lemon - 1

For Seasoning:

Oil - ½ tsp.
Mustard - ¼ tsp.
Asafoetida Powder - 2 pinches

Method:

1. Grind chillies, coconut, finely cut ginger along with salt in a mixie to a coarse paste.

2. Add coconut along with little water, and grind once.

3. Mix grated 'Tofu' at the end and grind just once lightly.

4. Take it in a vessel and squeeze lemon to that.

5. Heat oil, add mustard, allow to crackle, mix asafoetida in that oil and then pour over chutney.

Variation: Omit ginger, add ½ tsp. cumin seeds and grind.

Note: By adding Soya paneer (Tofu) to chutney less coconut can be used. Do not use more Tofu in chutney, otherwise chutney becomes slimy.

Tbl.sp. = Table Spoon
tsp. = Teaspoon

4. Urad Coconut Chutney

Ingredients:

Red chillies - 6
Urad dhal - 1½ Tbl.sps.
   (dehusked black gram dhal)
Grated fresh Coconut - ¼ cup
Garlic - 5 flakes
Salt - as required
Tamarind - Small Gooseberry
       sized (Soak in little water)
Oil - as required

For seasoning:

Oil - ½ tsp.
Curry leaves - 2 springs
Mustard seeds - ½ tsp.

Method:

1. Heat ½ tsp. of oil in a Kadai. Add red chillies, urad and roast until dhal turns golden.

2. Add garlic, coconut, at the end and fry until coconut turns to a pink colour.

3. Allow to cool and grind coarsely with salt and soaked tamarind.

4. Heat ½ tsp. of oil, season mustard seeds & curry leaves in that oil and add to chutney.

5. Serve with Idli/dosa or pongal.

Variation:

1. Omit garlic and grind as usual.

2. Do not roast coconut, omit garlic. Roast chillies & Urad alone. Add fresh coconut and grind with other ingredients.

Note: This chutney can be served with cooked rice as thuvayal.

5. Coconut Tomato Chutney

Ingredients:

Grated fresh coconut - ½ cup
Roasted gram - 1½ Tbl.sps.
Green chillies - 5
Tomatoes - 2 (Cut finely)
Finely cut onions - ¼ cup
Red chillies - 2
Mustard seeds - ½ tsp.
Oil - for frying, seasoning
Salt - as required (¾ tsp.)
Turmeric Powder - ½ tsp.

Method:

1. Grind coconut, chillies, roasted gram, salt and tomato together to a coarse paste.

2. Heat little oil in a kadai add mustard & broken red chillies.

3. Add onion and fry until golden.

4. Mix diluted ground paste to this along with turmeric powder.

5. Allow to boil once and remove from fire.

6. Serve either with Idli or dosa.

6. Onion Coconut Chutney

Ingredients:

Grated fresh Coconut - ½ cup
Tamarind - Gooseberry sized
                    (soak in little water)
Roasted gram - 1 cup
Big onions - 2
Salt - as required
Red chillies - 5
Oil - For seasoning
Mustard seeds - ¼ tsp.
Urad dhal - ½ tsp.

Method:

1. Peel and dice onions.

2. Grind coconut, chillies, roasted gram, salt and soaked tamarind to a paste.

3. Add onion at the end and grind coarsely.

4. Heat little oil, add mustard, urad fry until done and pour over chutney.

5. Serve with Idli, dosa, uttappam, adai or paniyaram varieties.

7. Roasted Chutney

Ingredients:

Red chillies - 7
Bengal gram dhal - 1 Tbl.sp.
Urad dhal - 1½ Tbl.sps.
Asafoetida - a pinch
Grated fresh coconut - ½ cup
Salt - as required
Tamarind - Small gooseberry sized
(soak in water)
Oil - 1 tsp.
Mustard seeds - ¼ tsp.
Curry leaves - 1 spring

Method:

1. Fry red chillies, bengal gram dhal, urad dhal in little oil until golden.

2. Add coconut at the end, fry until it turns to light pink.

3. Remove from fire and allow to cool.

4. Grind it along with tamarind, asafoetida to a coarse paste.

5. Heat little oil, fry mustard seeds, curry leaves and add to chutney.

6. Serve with Idli, dosa, adai varieties.

8. White Chutney

Ingredients:

Grated fresh Coconut - 1 cup
Green chillies - 3
Salt - ½ tsp., Oil - 1 tsp.
Mustard seeds - ¼ tsp.
Curry leaves - 2 springs
Asafoetida - 2 pinches
Broken red chilli - 1

Method:

1. Grate white portion alone from coconut. (Use coconut water for grinding instead of water)

2. Add green chillies, salt to the coconut and grind to a coarse chutney using just enough water / coconut water.

3. Heat little oil, add mustard seeds allow to splutter.

4. Mix curry leaves, asafoetida and broken red chilli in that oil and then pour over ground chutney.

5. Mix well and serve with Idli, dosa, aappam varieties.

   Note: 1. Use less green chillies for this chutney which gives better taste. 2. Add 1 diced big onion or few peeled small onions while grinding. (raw/fried)

Onion Based Chutney Varieties
9. Onion Chutney (For Ragai Dosa)

Ingredients:

Large Onions - 5
        (approximately ½ kg,)
Red chillies - 6
Tamarind - Gooseberry sized
        (soak in water)
Grated Jaggery - as required
Salt - 1 tsp.

For Seasoning:

Oil - 1 Tbl.sp.
Mustard seeds - ¼ tsp.
Curry leaves - 2 springs

Method:

1. Peel and dice onions to 1 inch pieces.

2. Dry roast red chillies until it turns crisp and dark brown in colour.

3. Add salt to roasted chillies in mixie and powder it.

4. Add grated jaggery and soaked tamarind to that and grind to a paste.

5. Mix Onions to that and grind coarsely.

6. Heat oil in a 'Kadai', add mustard seeds, curry leaves, and then add ground paste.

7. Fry for few minutes or until raw flavour of onion is lost.

8. Serve with Ragi dosa/idli.

Variation: Omit frying process. Grind red chillies as it is along with 1Tbl.sp. of roasted gram and 2 teaspoons of grated fresh coconut along with salt and Tamarind. Add onion at the end and grind. Follow the procedure as in the point 6 and 7.

1 tsp. = 5 gms (level measure)
1 Tbl.sp. = 15 gms = 3 tsps.

10. Small Onion Garlic Chutney

Ingredients:

Peeled small onion - 1 cup
    (approximately 200 gms.)
Peeled garlic - 10 flakes
Red chillies - 7
Grated fresh coconut - 1 Tbl.sp.
Tamarind - Gooseberry sized
Oil - for frying

For Seasoning:

Oil - 1 tsp.
Mustard seeds - ¼ tsp.
Curry leaves - 1 spring
Asafoetida - 2 pinches

Method:

1. Heat a teaspoon of oil and fry red chillies until crisp.

2. Take out and keep it aside in a plate.

3. Add little more oil in the kadai, and fry garlic and onion until transparent.

4. Allow everything to obtain room temperature.

5. Grind roasted, fried ingredients along with coconut, salt, tamarind to a coarse consistency.

6. Heat little oil separately add seasonings and then mix with chutney.

7. Serve this chutney with dosa varieties and Paniyaram Varieties.

Variation:

1. Instead of peeled small onions, use diced big onions in the above recipe.

2. Use 50% small onion and 50% big onion and fry both before grinding.

11. Roasted Chilli Onion Chutney

Ingredients:

Long red chillies - 10
Onions - ½ kg. (diced)
Peeled garlic - 2 flakes
Salt - as required
Oil - ½ tsp.

Method:

1. Heat oil in a 'Kadai' and fry red chillies in that until chillies turn into dark brown in colour.

2. Break the chillies into two or three pieces and put it in the mixie along with salt, garlic and diced onions.

3. Grind to a coarse chutney consistency.

4. Serve with Idli, dosa or paniyaram.

Options:

1. Crackle little mustard seeds in oil and add to chutney.

2. Instead of large onions use peeled small onions.

3. Add 2 springs of curry leaves while frying chillies.

4. Fry garlic, onions in oil and then grind.

   Note: Different taste of this chutney depends upon over roasted chilli only. So roast it until dark in colour.

12. Spicy Raw Onion Chutney

Ingredients:

Big Onions - 4
Long red chillies - 12
Tamarind - Small lemon sized
Salt - 1 Tbl.sp.
Sugar - ½ tsp. (optional)

For seasoning:

Oil - 2 Tbl.sps.
Mustard seeds - ½ tsp.

Method:

1. Peel and dice onions.
2. Soak red chillies, tamarind in water separately for ½ an hour.
3. Squeeze chillies from water and put it in mixie.
4. Add soaked tamarind, salt, sugar in that and grind it lightly.
5. Add ¼th of the onions in that and grind nicely.
6. Add rest of the onions and grind to a coarse paste.
7. Transfer the chutney in a bowl.
8. Heat oil, add mustard seeds, allow to crackle and add to chutney.
9. Serve with dosa, idli, paniyaram.
10. This chutney can be kept in refrigerator for 15 minutes.

Note: As this chutney is very spicy, more oil, salt, chillies, tamarind is used. Use very little chutney while eating. For children and those who are interested add little melted ghee on top of chutney while eating.

13. Onion Miriyam (Dosa Topping)

Ingredients:

Spicy Raw Onion Chutney -
1½ tsps. (Recipe No. 12)
*Andhra dhal powder - 1½ Tbl.sp.
Fresh thick curds - 1 ladle full

Method:

1. Mix dhal powder, chutney with curds to form a paste.
2. Apply this on top of dosa after toasting it both sides.
3. Serve immediately.

* Andhra dhal powder:

Prepared and sold by MHP masala (Mallika Home products)

This dhal powders in generally served with cooked hot rice. Same can be used to enhance taste of any vegetable porial. Sprinkle on top of porial just before removing from fire.

14. Fried Onion Chutney

Ingredients:

Big Onions - ½ kg.
Red chillies - 10
Tamarind - Small gooseberry sized
(soaked in water)
Grated Jaggery - Little
Salt - as required
Grated fresh Coconut - 2 tsps.
Roasted gram - 1 Tbl.sp.
Turmeric Powder - ¼ tsp.
Asafoetida - Little
Oil - 2 Tbl.sps.
Mustared seeds - ½ tsp.
Curry leaves - 2 springs

Method:

1. Peel and dice onions.
2. Grind red chillies, salt, jaggery, coconut, tamarind and roasted gram together in a mixie.
3. Add onions at the end and grind coarsely.
4. Heat oil in a pan, add mustard seeds, curry leaves, asafoetida and then ground paste.
5. Stir fry for few minutes.
6. Serve with oothappam, dosa varieties.

15. Coriander Lemon Chutney

Ingredients:

Coriander leaves - 2 bunches
Green chillies - 3
Cumin seeds - ½ tsp.
Salt - 1 tsp.
Ginger - 2 inch piece
Roasted gram - 1½ tsps.
Lemon - ½

For seasoning:

Oil - 1 tsp.
Mustard seeds - ½ tsp.

Method:

1. Wash coriander properly and then cut.
2. Scrape ginger and grind it with chillies, cumin and salt.
3. Add roasted gram and grind properly.
4. Mix coriander leaves at this stage and grind to a coarse chutney.
5. Squeeze lemon juice to that.
6. Heat oil, add mustard and mix with chutney

Variation:

1. Omit lemon, add soaked tamarind.
2. Use roasted, dehusked peanuts instead roasted gram.

16. Coriander Ginger Chutney

Ingredients:

Coriander leaves -1 bunch
Ginger - 1 inch piece
Green chillies - 3
Tomatoes - 3, Salt - as required
Grated fresh coconut - ½ cup
Asafoetida - 2 pinches

For Seasoning:

Oil - 1 tsp.
Mustard seeds - ¼ tsp.
Cumin seeds - ¼ tsp.

Method:

1. Wash and cut coriander leaves along with its stem into 2 or 3 pieces.
2. Cut tomatoes, remove outer skin from ginger and cut.
3. Grind all the mentioned ingredients to a coarse chutney consistency.
4. Heat little oil and season mustard and cumin seeds in it and pour over chutney.
5. Serve with Idli, dosa or pongal.

17. Coriander Garlic Chutney

Ingredients:

Coriander leaves - 2 big bunches
Green chillies - 10
Ginger - 1 inch piece
Garlic - 4 flakes
Salt - as required
Roasted gram - 1 Tbl.sp.

Method:

1. Wash and cut coriander leaves.
2. Add peeled garlic, ginger, chillies, salt and roasted gram to that.
3. Grind to a thick paste.
4. Use this for bhel puri, chat varieties, like potato bhel, puffed rice chat etc.,

18. Sour Coriander Chutney

Ingredients:

Peeled small onions - 10
Green chillies - 3
Coriander leaves - 1 bunch
Tamarind -
    Small gooseberry sized
Salt - as required

For seasoning:

Oil - 1 tsp.
Mustard seeds - ¼ tsp.

Method:

1. Grind all the mentioned ingredients together to coarse paste.
2. Heat little oil, add mustard, allow to splutter and add to chutney.
3. Serve with pongal, pesarattu, or kancheevaram idli.

Variation:

1. Add little grated jaggery while grinding.
2. Few springs of curry leaves can also be added while grinding.

19. Spicy Coriander Chutney

Ingredients:

Coriander leaves - 1 bunch
Green chillies - 5 (cut into two)
Peeled garlic - 3 flakes
Cumin seeds - ½ tsp.
Grated fresh coconut - ½ cup
Salt - as required
Finely cut onions - ¼ cup
Lemon - 1, Oil - for frying

Method:

1. Heat little oil in a kadai, add cumin seeds, peeled garlic, cut green chillies and fry for a minute.
2. Add grated coconut and remove from fire.
3. Add salt, coriander leaves to that and grind to a coarse chutney consistency.
4. Mix finely cut raw onions, and squeezed lemon juice to that.
5. Serve with Idli, dosa varieties.

Variation: 1. Omit lemon, add tamarind juice to that. 2. Add ginger instead of garlic. 3. Use mint leaves along with coriander while grinding.

Mint Chutney Varieties
20. Mint Lemon Chutney (For Sandwiches)

Ingredients:

Mint leaves - 1 cup
Scraped ginger - 1 inch piece
Green chillies - 3
Cumin seeds - 1 tsp.
Diced big onion - 1
Salt - as required, Lemon - 1

Method:

1. Remove leaves alone from stalks of mint, wash well.
2. Add ginger, chillies, cumin, onion, salt and grind to a smooth, thick paste with minimum possible water.
3. Squeeze lemon to that and mix well.
4. Use it as a sandwich spread.

Variation:

1. Omit onion and lemon. Instead add 1 Tbl.sp. of dry, sour pomegranate seeds (available in leading stores as anardhana) and grind.
2. Take equal quantities of mint and coriander leaves for grinding.
3. Omit cumin seeds add 1 tsp. of dhania (Coriander seeds) and grind along with other ingredients.

14

21. Spicy Mint Chutney (Cutlet)

Ingredients:

Mint leaves - 1½ cups
Green chillies - 3
Garlic - 2 flakes
Sugar - 1 tsp.
Salt - as required
Lemon Juice - 1 Tbl.sp.

Method:

1. Wash mint leaves well, and grind with other ingredients to a fine, smooth paste.

2. Add little water to dilute it.

3. Serve along with cutlet, tikkis, kababs, rolls, paratha's etc.,

22. Mint Ginger Chutney

Ingredients:

Mint leaves - 1 small bunch
Coriander leaves - 1 bunch
Ginger - 1 inch piece
Onion - 1 (diced)
Green chillies - 5
Tamarind - Small Gooseberry
            sized (soaked in water)
Salt - as required
Sugar - ½ tsp.

Method:

1. Clean mint, coriander leaves and then wash well.

2. Grind it with ginger, green chillies, onion, tamarind, salt, sugar to smooth paste.

3. Serve with idli or dosa varieties.

23. Mint Tomato Chutney

Ingredients:

Mint leaves - 1 cup
Peeled small onions - 10
Tomato - 2 (diced)
Urad dhal - 1 Tbl.sp.
      (de husked black gram)
Green chillies (Chopped) - 5
Grated fresh coconut - 2 Tbl.sps.
Tamarind - Small Gooseberry
      sized (soaked in water)
Salt - Little
Oil - For roasting and seasoning

For seasoning:

Mustard seeds - ¼ tsp.
Asafoetida - 2 pinches

Method:

1. Roast urad dhal with ½ tsp. of oil until golden.

2. Add coconut at the end, fry until it changes its colour. Take out from fire and transfer to a plate.

3. Heat another teaspoon of oil in that same 'kadai' and fry chopped green chillies, small onions and then mint leaves, tomatoes.

4. Fry until moisture is evaporated and allow to cool thoroughly.

5. Add salt, tamarind to that and grind all the roasted, fried ingredients together to chutney consistency.

6. Heat ½ tsp. of oil add mustard seeds, allow to crackle, add asafoetida in that hot oil and add to chutney.

7. Mix well and serve with Idli, dosa varieties.

24. Mint Garlic Chutney

Ingredients:

Red chillies - 4
Bengal gram dhal - 1 Tbl.sp.
Green chillies - 2
Big Onion - 1 (diced)
Tomatoes - 2 (diced)
Peeled garlic - 3 flakes
Tamarind - Small gooseberry sized
        (soaked in water)
Salt - as required
Cumin seeds - ½ tsp.
Grated fresh coconut - ¼ cup
Oil - for frying

Method:

1. Heat ½ teaspoon of oil, add red chillies, bengal gram dhal and fry until golden. Take out and transfer to a plate.

2. In the same kadai, heat little oil add garlic, onion, chopped green chillies and then tomatoes.

3. Fry until moisture evaporates, add mint leaves, fry for a minute and remove from fire.

4. Mix all roasted, fried ingredients with salt, cumin, tamarind, coconut and grind to chutney consistency.

25. Mint Coconut Chutney

Ingredients:

Mint leaves - 1 cup
Grated fresh coconut - ¼ cup
Red chillies - 3, Big Onion - 1
Salt - as required
Tamarind - Small gooseberry
        sized (soaked in water)
Oil - for frying
Mustard seeds - ¼ tsp.

Method:

1. Pluck the leaves alone from mint, measure, wash well and grind it with red chillies, coconut, salt, onion and tamarind to a smooth paste.

2. Heat oil in a 'kadai' add mustard seeds, allow to crackle and fry the ground chutney for few minutes.

3. Serve with Idli or dosa varieties.

26. Mint Onion Chutney

Ingredients:

Peeled small onions - 1 cup
Mint leaves - 2 bunches
        (pluck & wash)
Green chillies - 4 (cut into pieces)
Red chillies - 3
Ginger - 1 inch piece
Peeled Garlic - 5 flakes
Grated fresh coconut - ½ cup
Tomato - 2 (diced)
Bengal gram dhal - 1½ Tbl.sp.
Cumin seeds - 1 tsp.
Salt - as desired
Tamarind - Small gooseberry sized
Oil - for frying
Mustard seeds - ¼ tsp.
Asafoetida - 2 pinches

Method:

1. Heat ½ tsp. of oil in a kadai and fry red chillies, bengal gram dhal and cumin seeds.

2. Fry garlic, onions, green chillies, tomato, mint, separately using little oil.

3. To all roasted, fried ingredients add rest of the mentioned ingredients and grind to chutney consistency.

4. Heat little oil, add mustard seeds, allow to crackle, add asafoetida and mix with chutney.

5. Serve with idli, dosa varieties.

27. Mint Mango Chutney

Ingredients:

Plucked mint leaves - 1 cup
Sour raw mango -
        ½ peeled & sliced
Green chillies - 4
Grated fresh coconut - ¼ cup
Scraped ginger - ½ inch piece
Salt - as desired

Method:

1. Wash mint leaves well and grind with all other mentioned ingredients to a smooth paste using minimum water possible.

2. Use as a sandwich spread.

Variation:

1. Use equal quantities of coriander and mint.

2. Omit coconut and grind rest of the ingredients.

28. Mint Coconut Garlic Chutney

Ingredients:

Grated fresh coconut - ½ cup
Mint leaves - 1 cup
Roasted gram - 1½ Tbl.sp.
Peeled garlic - 5 flakes
Chopped Green chillies - 5
Salt - as required
Tamarind - Small gooseberry sized
                (soaked in water)
Oil - for frying / seasoning
Mustard seeds - ¼ tsp.

Method:

1. Heat little oil and fry green chillies, garlic and then mint leaves.

2. Add other ingredients and grind to coarse chutney consistency.

3. Season mustard seeds in little oil and add to chutney.

   Note: Reduce or increase the quantity of garlic depending upon its size.

   Green chillies: Depending upon the size and hotness of chilli alter the measurement according to individual taste.

29. Spicy Mint Coriander Chutney

Ingredients:

Mint leaves - 4 small bunches
Coriander leaves -
                1 medium bunch
Green chillies - 5
Dhania (Coriander seeds) - ½ tsp.
Big Onion - 1 (diced)
Grated fresh coconut - 2 Tbl.sps.
Salt - as required, Oil - Little

For seasoning:

Mustard seeds - ½ tsp.

Method:

1. Clean, pluck and wash mint, coriander leaves well in water.

2. Heat ½ tsp. of oil in a 'kadai', add chopped chillies, mint and fry until mint shrinks.

3. Grind with all other mentioned ingredients to smooth chutney consistency.

4. Heat little oil, add mustard seeds allow to crackle and mix with chutney.

5. For better taste, squeeze little lemon juice.

6. Serve with cutlet, aloo tikki, samosa varieties.

Note: For this chutney onion should be added raw. Those who do not like raw taste of onion, can fry onion and grind with other ingredients.

30. Mint Dhal Chutney

Ingredients:

Mint leaves - 1 bunch
Coriander leaves - ½ bunch
Ginger - 1 inch piece
Peeled garlic - 3 flakes
Green chillies - 5
Thuar dhal - 1½ tsp.
Salt - 1 tsp., Sugar - 1 tsp.
Lemon - 1, Oil - for seasoning
Mustard seeds - ½ tsp.

Method:

1. Roast thuar dhal in ¼ tsp. of oil until golden.
2. Pluck, wash coriander, mint leaves properly.
3. Peel, chop ginger and garlic into pieces.
4. Powder roasted dhal in mixie and then add rest of the ingredients and grind to chutney consistency.
5. Squeeze lemon at the end.
6. Heat little oil and season mustard seeds in it. Add to chutney and mix well.

31. Mint Anardhana Chutney

Ingredients:

Mint leaves - 1 bunch
Coriander leaves - ½ bunch
Green chillies - 6
Salt - ¾ tsp.
Dry, sour Pomegranate seeds -
            1 Tbl.sp. (Anardhana)

Method:

1. Wash mint, coriander leaves properly.
2. Grind with chillies, salt and pomegranate seeds to chutney consistency.
3. Use as a sandwich spread.

Beginners Tip: Always wash leafy vegetables by rinsing it in water which is kept at a larger vessel. The mud which is sticking to the leaves settle down in water. Do not wash it under running tap water.

32. Mint Kopra Chutney (For Cutlet)

Ingredients:

Mint leaves - 1 bunch
Red chillies - 4
Grated dry coconut - 1 Tbl.sp.
Soaked Tamarind -
            Small gooseberry sized
Salt - as required, Oil - for frying
Finely cut large onion - 1

Method:

1. Pluck and wash mint leaves.
2. Grind it with chillies, salt, dry coconut and tamarind to smooth paste.
3. Heat oil in a pan and fry onions for 1 or 2 minutes.
4. Add ground paste and fry well.
5. Serve with cutlets.

33. Mint Coriander Chutney

Ingredients:

Plucked mint leaves - 1 cup
Coriander leaves - 1 bunch
Dhania - 1 tsp.
Tamarind - Small gooseberry sized
Grated Jaggery - 1 Tbl.sp.
Green chillies - 5
Diced big onion - 1
Grated fresh coconut - 2 Tbl.sps.
Oil - little, Mustard seeds - ½ tsp.
Asafoetida Powder - 2 pinches

Method:

1. Wash mint, coriander leaves in enough water properly.
2. Grind it with tamarind, dhania, chillies, onion, salt and coconut to coarse chutney consistency.
3. Heat oil, add mustard seeds, allow to crackle, mix asafoetida powder and then pour on top of chutney, mix well.

34. Hotel Mint Chutney

Ingredients:

Mint leaves - 2 cups
Green chillies - 3, Salt - 1 tsp.
Peeled small onions - 2
Lemon - 1, Sugar - 1 tsp.
Fresh thick curds - ¼ cup

Method:

1. Wash mint leaves and grind it with green chillies, onion, salt, sugar to a thick paste.
2. Squeeze lemon juice while grinding so that green colour of chutney is retained.
3. Strain curds through a fine mesh strainer to remove excess moisture and then whip it.
4. Mix with ground mint chutney.
5. Serve with all fried foods. Ex: Spring rolls, Wontons, Samosa's etc.,

Variation: 1. Omit lemon juice, instead add little sour green mango and grind the chutney. 2. Omit onion, add 2 flakes of garlic. 3. Instead of small onion, add 1 peeled, diced big onion. 4. Mix 1 Tbl.sp. of vinegar instead of lemon juice.

35. Mint Pani puri Chutney

Ingredients:

Mint leaves - 1 cup
Coriander leaves - ½ bunch
Green chillies - 3, Lemon - 1 or 2
Cumin seeds - ½ tsp. Sugar - 1 tsp.
Black salt - 1 tsp. (powdered)
Powdered salt - ½ tsp.

Method:

1. Wash mint, coriander leaves properly and grind it with chillies, cumin, salt, black salt and sugar to a smooth paste.
2. Mix lemon juice to the chutney.
3. Separately keep half of the thick chutney for mixing bhel-puri.
4. To the rest of the chutney mix approximately 5 cups of water and strain it through fine-mesh strainer.
5. Taste and adjust quantity of salt.
6. Serve as pani to pour in pani-puri.

Variation: Omit lemon juice. Instead add little soked tamarind while grinding.

Garlic Chutney Varieties
36. Garlic Chutney

Ingredients:

Peeled Garlic - 15 flakes
Red chillies - 2
Grated fresh coconut - 1½ Tbl.sp.
Salt - as required

Method:

1. In small mixie break chillies and put it.

2. Put peeled garlic, salt, coconut on top and grind to coarse paste.

3. No need to season this.

4. Serve with paniyaram, adai and dosai varieties.

Note: As this is very strong flavoured chutney serve small quantities. Garlic is added raw in the chutney for maximum benefit of heart patients.

37. Garlic, Curry leaves Chutney

Ingredients:

Peeled Garlic - 20 flakes
Red chillies - 8
Cumin seeds - ¼ tsp.
Curry leaves - 2 springs
Salt - as desired
Asafoetida - as desired
Tamarind - Small gooseberry sized
(soaked in water)

Method:

1. Soak tamarind in little water for 10 minutes.

2. Grind red chillies, tamarind, salt, curry leaves and cumin seeds to a smooth paste.

3. Add garlic at the end and grind to a coarse paste.

4. Serve with dosa, adai, roti varieties.

38. Maharastra Garlic Chillies Chutney

Ingredients:

Red chillies - 10
Peeled Garlic - 6 flakes
Cumin seeds - 5 tsps.
Dhania - 5 tsps.
Bengal gram dhal - ¼ cup
Salt - as desired

Method:

1. Fry red chillies in little oil and keep aside.

2. Fry garlic in little oil and keep aside.

3. Dry roast cumin, dhania, bengal gram dhal separately until golden in colour.

4. Mix salt with all roasted, fried ingredients and powder it in a mixie.

5. Store it in a bottle.

6. Whenever required take required quantity, mix with little water to chutney consistency and serve.

Variation: Sesame seeds chutney: Omit bengal gram dhal. Roast sesame seeds instead of that. Prepare as mentioned in the above recipe.

39. Garlic Spicy Chutney

Ingredients:

Peeled Garlic - 15 flakes
Red chillies - 8, Salt - as desired
Lemon - 1, Oil - 1 Tbl.sp.
Mustard seeds - ¼ tsp.
Cumin seeds - ¼ tsp.

Method:

1. Soak red chillies in enough water for 15minutes.
2. Squeeze chillies from water, add salt, garlic and grind to a smooth, thick paste.
3. Heat little oil in a 'kadai', season mustard, cumin seeds and then add ground paste.
4. Fry until raw flavour of garlic is lost.
5. Switch off the stove, squeeze lemon juice and mix well.
6. As this is very spicy serve in very small quantities along with idli, dosa varieties.

Variation: 1. Reduce garlic to 7 flakes, add 3 big onions and grind to paste. 2. Omit lemon, instead add little soaked tamarind and grind. 3. Do not fry the chutney. Can be served raw. Use more oil for seasoning. 4. Roast chillies in little oil, powder it along with salt in small mixie then add garlic, water and grind to paste. 5. Reduce chillies, add little grated coconut and grind to chutney consistency.

40. Garlic Mint Chutney

Ingredients:

Peeled Garlic - 12 flakes
Big Onion - 1 diced
Green chillies - 6
Mint leaves - ½ bunch
Salt - Little

Method:

1. Grind all the mentioned ingredients together to coarse chutney consistency.
2. Serve with idli, dosa varieties. No need to season this.

41. Garlic Horse Gram Chutney

Ingredients:

Horse Gram - ¼ cup
Red chillies - 4
Peeled Garlic - 20 flakes
Salt - as required
Grated fresh coconut - 2 Tbl.sps.

Method:

1. Dry roast horse gram in a 'kadai' until it changes its colour.
2. Powder it in a small mixie.
3. Add red chillies, garlic, salt, coconut along with little water and grind to a coarse chutney consistency.
4. Serve with Ragi roti, dosa, idli varieties.

Variation: After dry roasting horse gram, rub well with hands to remove outer skin. Use only 2 flakes of garlic and grind it as horse gram chutney. Adjust chillies, salt according to individual taste.

Note: More garlic is used in this chutney. As garlic has more medicinal value, this chutney can be served for Heart patients, Diabetes patients and obese persons. Garlic helps to reduce cholestral in blood.

Dhal Chutney Varieties
42. Thuar dhal Garlic Chutney

Ingredients:

Thuar dhal - 2 Tbl.sps.
    (Dehusked, split red gram dhal)
Grated fresh coconut - ½ cup
Red chillies - 8
Tamarind - 1 inch piece
            (Soaked in water)
Grated Jaggery - little
Peeled Garlic - 8 flakes
Salt - as required, Oil - 2 tsps.
Mustard seeds - ½ tsp.

Method:

1. Roast chillies and thuar dhal using ¼ tsp. of oil until dhal turns golden brown.
2. Fry garlic in little oil separately.
3. Grind both with coconut, salt, tamarind, Jaggery to coarse chutney consistency.
4. Heat little oil, add mustard seeds, allow to crackle and mix with chutney.
5. Can serve with pongal, uppuma, dosa varieties and with cooked rice as thuvayal.

43. Bengal gram dhal Chutney

Ingredients:

Bengal gram dhal - ¼ cup
Grated fresh coconut - ½ cup
Green chillies - 6
Salt - as required
Oil - for frying, seasoning
Mustard seeds - ¼ tsp.

Method:

1. Heat little oil and fry bengal gram dhal until golden red in colour.
2. Allow to cool, add just enough water to cover and soak for 10 minutes.
3. Grind it with green chillies, salt and add coconut at the end. Grind to a coarse chutney consistency.
4. Season mustard seeds in oil and mix with chutney.
5. Serve with Idli, bonda, vadai varieties.

Variation: 1. Squeeze little lemon juice and mix with chutney. 2. Use roasted gram, instead of bengal gram dhal. Omit roasting process. 3. Add little thick butter milk after grinding the chutney.

44. Roasted gram Chutney

Ingredients:

Red chillies - 7
*Roasted Gram - 1 level cup
Grated fresh coconut - 2 tsps.
Peeled Garlic - 2 flakes
Salt - as required

For seasoning:

Oil - 1 tsp.
Mustard seeds - ¼ tsp.
Asafoetida - 2 pinches

*Roasted gram = puffed bengal
 gram = Pottukadali in Tamil

Method:

1. Grind all the mentioned ingredients with just enough water to coarse chutney consistency.
2. Dilute the chutney with more water to make it little watery. (To be served like that)
3. Heat little oil, season with mustard seeds, asafoetida and mix with chutney.
4. Serve with Idli, dosa varieties.

Note: In this chutney only very little coconut is added as a binding agent. Those patients who has to omit coconut in their diet as prescribed by doctors can prepare chutney like this everyday.

27

45. Roasted Peanut Chutney

Ingredients:

Roasted Peanuts - 1 cup
Green chillies - 6
Citric acid - 2 pinches
Salt - as required

For seasoning:

Oil - 1 tsp.
Mustard seeds - ¼ tsp.

Method:

1. De husk roasted nuts. Add salt, chillies, citric acid with that and grind to thick paste.

2. Put it in an air-tight container and keep it in refrigerator.

3. Whenever required take required quantity and dilute it with required water and then season with mustard seeds.

   Note: This chutney can be kept in refrigerator upto 1 month.

46. Roasted Peanut Garlic Chutney

Ingredients:

Roasted Peanuts
      (dehusked) - 1cup
Garlic - 2 flakes
Green chillies - 6
Salt - as required
Soaked Tamarind -
      Small gooseberry sized
Peeled small onion - 7
Oil - as required

For seasoning:

Mustard seeds - ½ tsp.
Urad dhal - 1 tsp.
Curry leaves - 2 springs

Method:

1. Grind peanuts with green chillies, salt, garlic and tamarind to coarse chutney consistency.

2. Add peeled small onion and grind at the end to coarse paste.

3. Heat oil add mustard seeds, urad dhal, curry leaves and mix with chutney.

Variation:

1. Reduce number of green chillies, add few red chillies and grind.

2. Omit small onion and grind.

47. Roasted Peanut Ginger Chutney

Ingredients:

Roasted Peanuts
    (De husked) - ½ cup
Red chillies - 4
Peeled Ginger - ½ inch piece
Lemon juice - 1 tsp.
Salt - as required
Oil - for seasoning
Mustard seeds - ¼ tsp.

Method:

1. Roast chillies alone using very little oil.
2. Add roasted peanuts, ginger and salt to that. Grind to coarse chutney consistency.
3. Add lemon juice and mix well.
4. Season mustard seeds in little oil and mix with chutney.

    Note: Grind this chutney to coarse consistency only. Then only this chutney tastes good. Use very small piece of ginger.

48. Thuar dhal Chutney

Ingredients:

Thuar dhal - ¼ cup
    (De hunsked split red gram)
Peeled small onions - 10
Red chillies - 8
Tamarind -
    Small gooseberry sized (soaked)
Salt - as required
Coriander leaves -½ bunch
Curry leaves - 2 springs
Ghee, Oil - as required
Mustard seeds - ¼ tsp.
Cumin seeds - ½ tsp.
Asafoetida - 2 pinches

Method:

1. Fry red chillies, thur dhal until golden brown using little ghee.
2. Transfer the roasted ingredients in a plate.
3. In that same frying pan fry small onions using little oil.
4. Grind roasted ingredients along with salt, tamarind, coriander, curry leaves until coarse chutney consistency.
5. Add fried onion at the end and grind again.
6. Season mustard, cumin in little oil, mix asafoetida powder in that hot oil itself and add to chutney.
7. Mix well and serve along with adai, dosai varieties.

49. Spicy Roasted gram Chutney (For Masal Dosai)

Ingredients:

Roasted gram - 1 cup
          (Pottu kadalai in tamil)
Red chillies - 12
Salt - ¾ tsp.
Tamarind (soaked) -
          Small gooseberry sized
Peeled small onions - 3
Curry leaves - 3 springs

Method:

1. In mixie jar first put roasted gram, chillies, salt and powder coarsely.

2. Add onion, curry leaves, tamarind and grind to a thick chutney consistency.

3. Use this chutney to spread on top of dosa and then keep potato masala inside.

Other Chutney Varieties
50. Cumin Chutney

Ingredients:

Red chillies - 5
Cumin seeds - 1½ Tbl.sps.
Peeled Garlic - 6 flakes
Big Onions - 3 (150 gms.)
Tamarind -
          Gooseberry sized (soaked)
Salt - as required
Grated Jaggery - as desired
Oil - For roasting & seasoning
Mustard seeds - ¼ tsp.
Curry leaves - 1 spring
Asafoetida - 2 pinches

Method:

1. Dry roast red chillies, cumin seeds without oil.

2. Peel garlic, dice onions and fry both using little oil.

3. Powder chillies, cumin, salt in mixie and then add fried garlic, onion.

4. Grind to coarse chutney consistency.

5. Heat little oil, season mustard seeds, curry leaves and then add asafoetida in that. Mix with chutney.

6. Serve with Idli, dosa, pongal varieties.

51. Sesame Seed Chutney

Ingredients:

*White sesame seeds - ¼ cup
Grated fresh coconut - ½ cup
Red chillies - 6, Salt - as required
Tamarind -
   Small gooseberry sized (soaked)
Jaggery - little
Curry leaves - 3 springs
Coriander leaves - ½ small bunch

White sesame seeds = Til = Ellu
in Tamil

Method:

1. Dry roast sesame seeds until it turns golden.

2. Allow to cool thoroughly.

3. Grind other mentioned ingredients to coarse chutney consistency, add roasted sesame at the end and grind again.

4. Serve with pongal/bonda varieties.

52. Sesame seed Pachidi

Ingredients:

White Sesame seeds - 2 Tbl.sps.
Red chillies - 5, Raw rice - 1½ tsp.
Tamarind - Lemon sized
Salt - 1 tsp., Oil - Little
Grated Jaggery - 1 Tbl.sp.
Mustard seeds - ¼ tsp.
Urad dhal - ½ tsp.
Curry leaves - 2 springs

Method:

1. Dry roast red chillies, sesame seeds and rice until golden brown.

2. Allow to cool and powder it in a mixie.

3. Soak tamarind in water and squeeze to get 1½ cups of extract.

4. Heat oil in a 'kadai' add mustard seeds, urad dhal, curry leaves and then pour tamarind extract.

5. Add salt, jaggery and allow to boil.

6. Add powdered ingredients and boil until thick, stirring in between.

7. Serve with rice uppuma, thuar dhal uppuma, medhu vadai etc.,

Variation: Omit rice in the roasting process. Mix rice flour in little water, add it at the end, boil until thick.

53. Bombay Chutney

Ingredients:

Big onions - 2, Green chillies - 5
Tomato - 1 (optional - diced)
Ginger - 1 inch piece
Curry leaves - 2 springs
Bengal gram flour - 2 Tbl.sps.
Water - 2 cups
Cumin seeds - ½ tsp.
Urad dhal - 1 tsp.
Turmeric powder - 1 tsp.
Salt - as required
Lemon - 1, Oil - 1 Tbl.sp.

Method:

1. Cut onions, tomatoes finely and green chillies into lengthwise pieces.
2. Scrape and grate ginger.
3. Mix water with bengal gram flour without forming lumps.
4. Heat oil in a 'kadai' and fry cumin seeds, urad dhal and then curry leaves.
5. Add green chillies, onion and fry until translucent.
6. Mix tomatoes and stir fry for few minutes.
7. Add grated ginger and then pour diluted bengal gram mixture in it.
8. Add salt, turmeric and stir constantly without forming lumps.
9. Cook until chutney becomes thick. Squeeze lemon juice, mix well and take out from fire.
10. Serve with puri or chappathi.

54. Dhania - Cumin Chutney

Ingredients:

Dhania - 1½ tsps.
Cumin seeds - 1 tsp.
Grated fresh coconut - ½ cup
Red chillies - 5, Onion - 1
Tamarind - Small gooseberry
                  sized (soaked)
Salt - as required, Oil - 1 tsp.
Mustard seeds - ¼ tsp.
Cumin seeds - ½ tsp.
Curry leaves - 1 spring

Method:

1. Cut onions finely.
2. Grind red chillies, dhania, cumin, salt, tamarind along with coconut to coarse chutney consistency.
3. Mix cut onions with that.
4. Season mustard, cumin, curry leaves in little oil and mix with chutney.
5. Serve with idli, dosa or pongal varieties.

Tomato Chutney Varieties
55. Tomato Chutney

Ingredients:

Large Onions - 2
Firm ripe tomatoes - ¼ kg.
Green chillies - 2, Oil - 1 Tbl.sp.
Red chilli powder - ½ tsp.
Sugar - 1 tsp., Salt - 1½ tsp.
Roasted gram powder - 1 Tbl.sp.
Garam masala powder - ½ tsp.
Mustard seeds - ¼ tsp.
Urad dhal - ½ tsp.
Curry leaves - 2 springs
Broken cashews - 10

Method:

1. Cut onions and tomatoes finely.

2. Slit chillies length wise.

3. Heat oil in a 'kadai' and add mustard, urad dhal, cashews, curry leaves.

4. Allow to splutter and add onions.

5. Fry until golden brown.

6. Add cut tomatoes fry for few minutes and mix salt, sugar, chilli powder, garam masala in that.

7. Pour little water and allow to cook for few minutes.

8. Allow the chutney to thicken and then sprinkle roasted gram powder. Mix well. Add chopped coriander leaves.

9. Serve with idli or chappathi.

Variation: 1 teaspoon of ginger-garlic paste can be added while frying onion.

56. Tomato Spicy Chutney

Ingredients:

Frim ripe Tomatoes - 8
Big Onions - 2
Ginger - 1 inch piece
        (peel and cut)
Peeled Garlic - 5 flakes
Green Chillies - 4
Salt - as required
Oil - for frying

Dry Roast and Powder:

Red chillies - 3
Dhania - 2 tsps.

Method:

1. Cut onions and tomatoes finely.
2. Heat oil in a 'kadai' and fry green chillies, garlic and then add onion, ginger.
3. Fry stirring constantly until onions turns transluscent.
4. Add tomatoes and fry until moisture is absorbed completely. Allow to cool thoroughly.
5. Mix salt and grind to smooth paste.
6. Add roasted chilli-dhania powder to that and mix well.
7. Serve with adai or vadai varieties.

57. Tomato Onion Chutney

Ingredients:

Large Onions - 2
Peeled small Onions - 1 cup
Ripe Tomatoes - 6 (½ kg.)
Peeled Garlic - 5 flakes
Red chillies - 8
Tamarind - Small gooseberry sized
Curry leaves - 2 springs
Salt - as required
Asafoetida - Little
Oil - Little
Mustard seeds - ½ tsp.
Urad dhal - 1 tsp.

Method:

1. Peel and dice onions.
2. Cut tomatoes finely.
3. Heat little oil in a 'kadai', add mustard, urad dhal, curry leaves and then garlic, small onion, large onion.
4. Fry well and then add tomatoes.
5. Stir fry until moisture is evaporated.
6. Add salt, tamarind and remove from fire.
7. Allow to cool thoroughly and grind to a coarse chutney consistency.
8. Serve with chettinad vellai appam.

58. *Tomato Coconut Chutney*

Ingredients:

Red Chillies - 6
Tomatoes - 2
Large Onions - 1
Coconut - ½
Salt - as required
Oil - for frying, seasoning

For Seasoning:

Mustard - ½ tsp.
Urad dhal - ½ tsp.
Asafoetida - Little

Method:

1. Peel and dice onion, and tomatoes.

2. Grate coconut.

3. Heat oil in a 'kadai' add mustard, urad dhal and then asafoetida, red chillies.

4. Add diced onion and fry well.

5. Mix diced tomatoes and fry until moisture evaporates.

6. Add coconut at the end and fry for 1 or 2 minutes.

7. Allow to cool thoroughly, add salt and grind to coarse chutney consistency.

8. Serve with Idli, dosai varieties.

Variation: Fry 1 onion, 1 tomato and grind it along with coconut, red chillies, salt. Add little tamarind while grinding. Season with mustard, urad dhal.

59. Chettinad Tomato Chutney

Ingredients:

Firm ripe Tomatoes - 10 (1 kg.)
Red chillies - 15
Peeled Garlic - 10 flakes
Peeled small Onions - 1 cup
Tamarind - Gooseberry sized
                (soaked)
Salt - as required
Oil - for frying / seasoning
Curry leaves - 2 springs
Coriander leaves - ¼ bunch
                (wash & chop)

For seasoning:

Mustard seeds - ½ tsp.
Urad dhal - 1 tsp.
Asafoetida powder - 2 pinches

Method:

1. Wash and cut tomatoes finely.

2. Heat little oil in a 'kadai' add red chillies, garlic and then onion.

3. Fry until onion turns transluscent and then add chopped tomatoes.

4. Stir until moisture evaporates.

5. Add curry leaves, coriander leaves and switch off the stove.

6. Mix soaked tamarind, salt and allow to cool thoroughly.

7. Grind to a coarse paste.

8. Heat little oil season mustard, urad, asafoetida and then mix with chutney.

9. Serve with chettinad vellai appam / vellai paniyaram / dosai varieties.

Note: Quantity of Garlic which is mentioned in this denotes small country garlic. If you are using hill garlic / china garlic reduce the quantity according to individual taste.

60. Tomato Coriander Chutney

Ingredients:

Ripe Tomatoes - ½ kg.
Coriander leaves - 2 big bunches
Peeled Garlic - 8 flakes
Ginger - 1½ inch piece
Red chillies - 10
Grated fresh coconut - ¼ cup
Salt - as desired
Oil - for frying

Method:

1. Remove thick stems from coriander, wash and chop.
2. Peel garlic, ginger and cut into convenient pieces.
3. Wash and dice tomatoes to medium sized square.
4. Heat little oil in a 'kadai', add red chillies, garlic, allow to turn golden and then mix tomatoes.
5. Stir fry until moisture evaporates.
6. Add coriander, coconut and fry for another few minutes.
7. Allow to cool, add ginger, salt and grind to coarse chutney consistency.
8. Serve with Idli, dosa, chappathi or puri varieties.

61. Tomato Masala Chutney

Ingredients:

Firm ripe Tomatoes -
      5 (Medium sized)
Peeled Garlic - 6 flakes
Peeled small onion - 10
Red chillies - 8
Tamarind - Gooseberry sized
      (soaked)
Grated Jaggery - Optional
Bengal Gram Dhal - 1 Tbl.sp.
Urad Dhal - 1 Tbl.sp.
      (Dehusked blackgram)
Cumin seeds - 1 tsp.
Cloves - 2
Aniseed - ½ tsp.
Salt - as required
Oil / ghee - for frying

Method:

1. Wash and dice tomatoes.

2. Heat ½ tsp. of ghee in a 'kadai', roast aniseeds, cloves until crip and powder separately.

3. Heat ½ tsp. of oil and roast red chillies, urad, bengal gram dhal and add cumin seeds at the end.

4. Fry until crisp and brown. Transfer it to a plate.

5. Heat little more oil in the same 'kadai' and fry garlic, onion, tomatoes.

6. Powder the roasted ingredients in a mixie, add fried vegetables along with salt, soaked tamarind.

7. Grind to coarse chutney consistency. Add spice powder at the end and run the mixie once again.

8. Transfer to a bowl and serve this chutney along with puri, chappathi, idli, paniyaram, dosai varieties.

62. Big Gooseberry Chutney

Ingredients:

Big Gooseberry - 3
Green Chillies - 5
Grated fresh coconut - 1 cup
Salt - as required
Oil - Little

For seasoning

Mustard seeds - ¼ tsp.
Urad dhal - ½ tsp.

Method:

1. Remove inner seed from gooseberries and cut into flakes.
2. Chop chillies into 2 or 3 pieces and then fry both in little oil.
3. Allow to cool thoroughly, add coconut, salt and grind to chutney consistency.
4. Heat little oil, add mustard, allow to splutter, and fry urad dhal, mix with chutney.

Variation: 1. To the above ground paste add ½ cup fresh thick curds and serve as a pachidi along with cooked rice. 2. ½ inch piece of ginger can be added while grinding. 3. Use 10 small gooseberries instead of 3 big gooseberries

63. Carrot Chutney

Ingredients:

Grated fresh carrot - 1 cup
Grated fresh coconut -
                 1½ Tbl. sps.
Red Chillies - 5
Bengal gram dhal - 1 Tbl.sp.
Urad dhal - 1 Tbl.sp.
Salt - as required
Tamarind - Small gooseberry
              sized (soaked)
Asafoetida - according to taste
Oil - for frying

Method:

1. Heat ½ tsp. of oil in a 'kadai' and roast red chillies, urad dhal, bengal gram dhal until golden and transfer to a plate.
2. In the same kadai pour little more oil and fry grated carrot until raw flavour is lost.
3. Allow to cool thoroughly.
4. Powder roasted ingredients along with salt in a mixie, add fried carrot, coconut, tamarind, asafoetida and grind to coarse chutney consistency.
5. No need to season this chutney. Serve with Idli, dosa varieties.

64. "Palak" Chutney

Ingredients:

Grated fresh Coconut - 1 cups
*Palak leaves - 15
Garlic - 2 flakes
Green Chillies - 4
Salt - according to taste
Lemon - ½
Oil for frving

Method:

1. Peel garlic, chop green chillies and fry both in little oil.

2. Add washed palak leaves (do not chop the leaves) and by fry until leaves shrink.

3. Allow to cool and grind it with coconut, salt to chutney consistency.

4. Squeeze lemon, mix well and serve with Idli, dosai, adai, chappathi, varieties.

* Palak = Spinach

65. Radish Chutney

Ingredients:

Peeled Small Onion - 1 cup
White radish
        cut into dices - 1 cup
Red Chillies - 6
Grated fresh coconut - ¼ cup
Salt - according to taste
Tamarind - Ssmall gooseberry
                sized (soaked)
Peeled Garlic - 1 flake
Asafoetida - according to taste
Oil - for frying / seasoning

For seasoning:

Mustard, Cumin,
        Curry leaves - little

Method:

1. Heat little oil in a 'kadai' and fry red chillies, onion, radish until radish turns brown.

2. Add grated coconut, fry for a minute and allow to cool thoroughly.

3. Mix salt, garlic, tamarind, asafoetida and grind to coarse chutney consistency.

4. Heat little oil season mustard, cumin and then curry leaves.

5. Add to chutney mix well and serve as chutney with Idli, dosa, chappathi varieties or as a thuvayal to cooked rice.

66. *White Radish, Coconut Chutney*

Ingredients:

Grated fresh coconut - ½ cup
Roasted gram - ¼ cup
Salt - as per taste
Grated Radish - ½ cup
Thick tamarind extract - 1 Tbl.sp.
Red chillies - 7
Asafoetida Powder - 2 pinches
Oil - for frying
Mustard - ¼ tsp.

Method:

1. Grind coconut, chillies, salt, roasted gram, asafoetida to a thick paste, with little water.

2. Add grated radish, grind coarsely, mix tamarind extract and transfer to a bowl.

3. Season mustard in little oil and mix with chutney.

4. Serve with Idli / dosa varieties.

67. *Chow-Chow Chutney*

Ingredients:

Finely cut chow-chow - 1 cup
Green Chillies - 4
Tamarind - Small gooseberry sized
(soaked)
Grated fresh coconut - ¼ cup
Salt - according to taste
Oil - for frying, seasonings

For seasoning:

Mustard - ¼ tsp.
Cumin seeds - ½ tsp.

Method:

1. Fry chow-chow pieces in little oil until it changes in colour.

2. Grind with other mentioned ingredients to coarse chutney consistency.

3. Heat little oil, season mustard, cumin and mix with chutney.

68. Mixed Vegetable Chutney

Ingredients:

Finely cut onion - ½ cup
Finely cut tomato - ¾ cup
Chopped chow-chow - ½ cup
Chopped carrot - ½ cup
Chopped knol-knol - ½ cup
Salt - according to taste
Grated fresh coconut - 2 Tbl.sps.
Oil - for frying
Chopped coriander,
        curry leaves - Little

Roast with little oil:

Red Chillies - 8
Bengal Gram dhal - 3 Tbl.sps.

For seasoning:

Mustard seeds - ¼ tsp.
Asafoetida powder - 2 pinches

Method:

1. Heat ½ tsp. of oil in a 'kadai' and roast chillies, bengal gram dhal until crisp, golden transfer to a plate.

2. In the same 'kadai' heat little oil and fry all the vegetables together (chow-chow, carrot, knol-knol) until raw flavour is lost.

3. Fry onion, tomatoes separately in little oil.

4. Powder roasted ingredients along with salt in the mixie.

5. Add all fried vegetables, coconut, coriander, curry leaves and grind to coarse chutney consistency.

6. Season mustard, asafoetida in little hot oil and mix with chutney.

69. Raw Tomato Chutney

Ingredients:

Raw, Country tomatoes - ¼ kg.
Onions - 2
Green chillies - 5
Salt - according to taste
Sugar - 1 tsp. (optional)

For seasing:

Mustard seeds - ¼ tsp.
Urad dhal - ¼ tsp.
Bengal gram dhal - ½ tsp.

Method:

1. Select raw tomatoes that has turned to little light green colour. (Just before riping consistency) Discard dark green ones.

2. Wash and chop it finely.

3. Cut onions and chillies finely.

4. Heat oil in a 'kadai' and fry chillies, onion, until it turns transluscent.

5. Add tomatoes and fry until moisture evaporate.

6. Allow to cool thoroughly and grind to coarse chutney consistency along with salt, sugar.

7. Heat little oil separately, season mustard, urad, bengal gram dhal and mix with chutney.

8. Serve with Idli, dosai, chappathi varieties.

Variation:

1. Add few peeled garlic while frying.

2. Do not grind. Add little water while frying and cook until pulpy. Serve.

3. Omit green chillies. Grind red chillies with little dry coconut. Add to chutney at the end of grinding.

70. Raw Tomato Coconut Chutney

Ingredients:

Raw tomatoes - ¼ kg.
Green chillies - 5
White sesame seeds - 2 tsps.
Grated fresh coconut - 2 Tbl.sps.
Salt - accorindg to paste
Oil - for frying
Mustard seeds - ¼ tsp.
Cumin seeds - ½ tsp.

Method:

1. Select raw country tomatoes which is just before riping stage. (Discard dark green ones which will not be tasty) wash and dice.

2. Cut green chillies into round pieces.

3. Heat very little oil, add sesame seeds, allow to fry, add coconut, green chillies and fry well.

4. Add tomatoes and fry until moisture evaporates.

5. Allow to cool, add salt and grind to coarse chutney consistency.

6. Heat little oil, add mustard, cumin allow to splutter and mix with chutney.

71. Neem Flower Chutney

Ingredients:

Dried neem flowers - 2 Tbl.sps.
Grated fresh coconut - ½ cup
Red chillies - 5
Garlic - 3 flakes
Salt - according to taste
Ghee - 1 tsp.
Sesame oil - 1 tsp.

Method:

1. Heat sesame oil in a frying pan and fry red chillies, garlic transfer to a plate.

2. In the same pan melt 1 teaspoon of ghee and fry dried neem flowers until it turns dark in colour.

3. Allow everything to cool thoroughly. Grind it together with coconut, salt to a coarse chutney consistency.

4. Serve with Idli.

Note: During neem flower season pick and wash them in luke warm water. Squeeze and soak in sour thick beaten curds to which little salt, lime juice are added. Allow to soak for 24 hours and dry under hot sun by spreading on a plastic sheet.

72. Curry Leaves Chutney

Ingredients:

Curry leaves - 1 cup
Coriander leaves - ½ bunch
Green chillies - 5
Ginger - ½ inch piece
Roasted gram - ½ Tbl.sp.
Salt - according to taste
Tamarind - Big goosebery sized
        (soaked)
Grated Jaggery - little
Oil - for seasoning
Mustard seeds - ¼ tsp.

Method:

1. Scrape ginger, wash curry leaves and coriander leaves properly.

2. Grind ginger, green chillies first in the mixie and then add soaked tamarind coriander, curry leaves, salt, jaggery, roasted gram and grind to a coarse chutney consistency.

3. Season mustard seeds in little oil and mix with chutney.

73. Raw Mango Coconut Chutney

Ingredients:

Raw salad mango - 1
        (*Bangaloora Mango)
Grated fresh coconut - ¼ cup
Red Chillies - 5
Fenugreek seeds - 2 tsps.
Mustard seeds - ¼ tsp.
Salt - according to taste
Grated Jaggery - 1 tsp.
Asafoetida powder - 2 pinches
Oil - Little
*Raw Mango - Kilimooku mangai
in Tamil

Method:

1. Dry roast red chillies, fenugreek and mustard lightly. (Do not over roast)

2. Scrape and grate mango.

3. Powder roasted ingredients along with salt in mixie.

4. Add jaggery, asafoetida, mango, coconut and then grind to a coarse chutney consistency. Serve. (No need to season this)

74. Raw Mango Garlic Chutney

Ingredients:

Raw salad mango - 1
Grated fresh coconut - ¼ cup
Peeled garlic - 3 flakes
Green chillies - 4
Salt - according to taste
Grated jaggery - 1 tsp.
Asafoetida Powder - 2 pinches
Oil - for frying
Mustard, Urad dhal - little

Method:

1. Select sweet and sour mango, peel skin and slice into thin broad pieces.

2. Grind garlic, green chillies first in mixie, add salt, jaggery, coconut, mango and then grind it to coarse chutney consistency.

3. Heat little oil, season mustard, urad dhal, asafoetida and mix with chutney.

75. Raw Mango Sweet - Sour Chutney

Ingredients:

Grated Raw Mango - 2 cups
Turmeric powder - ¼ tsp.
Ginger - 1 inch piece
Red chillies - 2
Red chilli powder - 1½ tsps.
Salt - according to taste
Sugar - 2 tsps.
Oil - 2 Tbl.sps.
Mustard Seeds - ½ tsp.
Curry leaves - 2 springs
Asafoetida Powder - 2 pinches

Method:

1. Scrape outer skin and grate ginger and mangoes separately.

2. Heat little oil in a 'kadai' add mustard, curry leaves, broken chillies and asafoetida.

3. Add grated ginger and then grated mangoes.

4. Mix turmeric powder, salt and fry until moisture evaporates.

5. Finally sprinkle sugar, red chilli powder and take out from stove, after mixing it well.

Variation: Omit red chillipowder. Grind green chillies and ginger together.

Note: If mangoes are sour, more sugar can be added.

76. Raw Mango Sweet - Spicy Chutney

Ingredients:

Raw Mangoes - 2
Red chillies - 4
Ginger - ½ inch piece
Sugar - 2 tsps.
Salt - according to taste
Turmeric powder - ¼ tsp.
Oil - as required

For seasoning:

Mustard seeds - ¼ tsp.
Fenugreek seeds - 2 pinches
Cumin seeds - 2 pinches
Curry leaves - 2 springs
Asafoetida Powder - 2 pinches

Method:

1. Scrape outer skin and slice mangoes into thin broad pieces.

2. Grind ginger, chillies together to a fine paste.

3. Heat oil in a 'kadai' add mustard, fenugreek, cumin seeds, curry leaves, asafoetida and then ground paste.

4. Fry for a minute and add sliced mangoes.

5. Stir for few minutes and pour little water. (Until mango pieces are immersed in that water)

6. Add salt, turmeric powder, sugar and boil until it reaches thick consistency.

77. Fenugreek leaves Chutney

Ingredients:

Fenugreek leaves - 1 bunch
Thuar dhal - 1 Tbl.sp.
Red chillies - 3, Pepper - ¼ tsp.
Cumin seeds - ¼ tsp.
Tomato - 1 diced
Grated fresh Coconut - 1 Tbl.sp.
Tamarind (soaked) -
          Small gooseberry sized
Mustard - ¼ tsp. Oil - little

Method:

1. Pluck fenugreek leaves alone from its stem and wash well in water. Strain and keep aside.

2. Heat ½ tsp. of oil in a 'kadai', add red chillies, thuar dhal, pepper, cumin and roast well. Transfer to a plate.

3. Fry fenugreek leaves, tomato separately in little oil.

4. Grind all roasted, fried ingredients together with coconut, tamarind, salt to coarse chutney consistency.

5. Season mustard in little oil and add to chutney.

Variation: Omit Fenugreek leaves. Use curry leaves and prepare chutney using same method as above.

78. Pumpkin Chutney

Ingredients:

Finely cut yellow pumpkin
pieces - 2 cups
Red chillies - 8, Oil - little
Bengal gram dhal - 1½ Tbl.sps.
Thuar dhal - 1½ Tbl.sps.
Salt - 1 level tsp.
Mustard seeds - ½ tsp.

Method:

1. Heat ½ tsp. of oil in a 'kadai' and fry red chillies, thuar dhal, bengal gram dhal until it turns golden brown.

2. Transfer roasted ingredients to a plate and heat another teaspoon of oil in that same 'kadai'.

3. Fry pumpkin pieces by sprinkling little water now and then.

4. Powder the roasted ingredients with salt in mixie and then add fried pumpkin pieces.

5. Grind to a coarse chutney consistency.

6. Season mustard in oil and add to chutney. Serve with dosa varieties.

79. Gherkins Chutney

Ingredients:

Grated fresh Coconut - ¾ cup
Salt - ¾ tsp.
Tamarind (soaked) -
Big gooseberry sized
Grated Jaggery - Little
Green chillies - 4
Asafoetida - 2 pinches
* Gherkins - 12
Big Onion - 1
Oil - Little
Mustard seeds - ½ tsp.
Cumin seeds - ¼ tsp.

* Gherkins = Kovaikai in tamil,
Dondakayi in Telugu

Method:

1. Cut onions and gherkins finely.

2. Heat little oil in a 'kadai', add mustard, cumin and then fry onion, gherkins.

3. Fry well until raw flavour of gherkin is lost.

4. Grind coconut, salt, jaggery, tamarind, chillies and asafoetida together to thick chutney consistency.

5. Add fried ingredients and grind very lightly. (Run the mixie at low speed at short intervals)

Note: This chutney tastes good if it is ground in a stone grinder (Ammi). **Caution:** Do not over grind, at the end. Gherkins should be fried properly, then only chutney tastes good.

80. Pineapple Chutney

Ingredients:

Firm ripe pineapple - 1 (small)
Red chillies - 8
Ginger - 1 inch piece
Urad dhal - 1 Tbl.sp.
Coriander leaves - 1 small bunch
Salt - according to taste
Oil - for frying / seasoning
Mustard seeds - ¼ tsp.
Lemon - 1

Method:

1. Remove outer skin, centre core and then cut pineapple to fine pieces.

2. Heat ½ tsp. of oil and roast red chillies and urad dhal until golden.

3. Transfer roasted ingredients in a plate and fry pineapple in the same 'kadai' using little oil.

4. Grind roasted ingredients along with salt in mixie, add coriander, pineapple and grind to coarse chutney consistency.

5. Squeeze lemon. Season mustard in little oil and mix with chutney.

   Note: If pineapple is little raw which is sour & sweet lemon can be omitted.

> *** Kadai = Curved fry pan**

81. Green Chilli Chutney

Ingredients:

Green chillies - 100 gms.
Tamarind - Big lemon sized
Salt - 2 tsps.
Sugar - 1 tsp. (optional)
Oil - 1 Tbl.sp.
Mustard seeds - ½ tsp.
Asafoetida powder - 2 pinches

Method:

1. Wash and chop chillies into 1 inch pieces.
2. Soak tamarind in water and squeeze to get thick extract.
3. Grind green chillies, with salt to a coarse paste.
4. Heat oil in a 'kadai' add mustard, allow to crackle, add asafoetida and then mix green chilli paste.
5. Fry for a minute, pour tamarind extract, sugar and boil until thick.
6. As this is very spicy serve in small quantities, along with pongal varieties.

82. Red Chilli Chutney

Ingredients:

Long red chillies - 5
Tamarind - Lemon sized
Peeled garlic - 3 flakes
Urad dhal - 1 tsp.
Salt - 1 tsp.
Oil - 2 tsp.
Mustard seeds - ¼ tsp.
Asafoetida - 2 pinches

Method:

1. Heat little oil in a kadai and roast chillies and urad dhal. Transfer to a plate.
2. Soak tamarind in water and prepare a thick extract.
3. Grind roasted ingredients along with salt, garlic, to a coarse paste.
4. Heat little oil, add mustard, asafoetida and ground paste.
5. Fry for a minute and pour tamarind extract.
6. Allow to boil and remove from fire.

83. Brinjal Onion Chutney

Ingredients:

Green brinjals - ¼ kg.
Peeled small onion - 10 (cut finely)
Tomato - 1
Soaked tamarind -
        Small gooseberry sized
Salt - according to taste
Oil - for frying / seasoning

Roast together:

Red Chillies - 5
Bengal Gram dhal   1½ tsp.

For seasoning:

Mustard, cumin seeds, Fenugreek
seeds - Little

Method:

1. Cut brinjals into fine pieces and keep immersed in water. Cut tomatoes finely.

2. Heat ½ tsp. oil in a 'kadai', roast chillies, bengal gram dhal and transfer to a plate.

3. In that same 'kadai' heat little more oil and fry cut onions, brinjal and stir fry until colour of brinjal changes.

4. Add tomatoes and stir until moisture evaporates.

5. Strain excess oil from brinjals and allow to cool.

6. Powder roasted ingredients in mixie first.

7. Add salt, tamarind, fried vegetables and grind to a coarse chutney consistency.

8. Heat little oil, add the mentioned ingredients, allow to splutter and pour over chutney.

9. Mix well and serve with Idli/dosa/pongal varieties.

84. Brinjal Chutney

Ingredients:

Country brinjals - ¼ kg.
Big Onions - 2, Red chillies - 6
Grated fresh coconut - 2 Tbl.sps.
Roasted gram - 2 tsps.
Salt - according to taste
Oil - for frying / seasoning
Mustard seeds - ¼ tsp.
Cumin seeds - ¼ tsp.

Method:

1. Cut brinjals into fine pieces and keep it immersed in water to prevent browning.
2. Cut onions finely.
3. Heat 2 Tbl.sp. of oil in a kadai and fry red chillies, onion and stir for few minutes.
4. Add brinjals and fry well. (until it changes colour)
5. Drain excess oil and allow to cool thoroughly.
6. Grind it along with coconut, salt and roasted gram to coarse chutney consistency.
7. Heat little oil, season mustard, cumin seeds and mix with chutney.
8. Serve with Idli / dosa varieties.

85. Brinjal Tomato Chutney

Ingredients:

Green brinjals - ¼ kg.
Green chillies - 5 (sliced)
Tomatoes - 2, Big onion - 1
Salt - according to taste
Coriander leaves - ½ bunch
Oil - for frying, seasoning
Mustard seeds - ¼ tsp.

Method:

1. Cut brinjals into very small pieces and keep it immersed in water to prevent browning.
2. Cut onions, tomatoes finely.
3. Heat little oil in a 'kadai', add onions, brinjals and fry well.
4. Add green chillies, tomatoes and stir until moisture evaporates.
5. Allow to cool thoroughly, add salt, coriander leaves and grind to a coarse chutney consistency.
6. Season mustard seeds in little oil and mix with chutney.
7. Serve with idli, dosa varieties.

86. Country Brinjal Chutney

Ingredients:

Red Chillies - 6
* Violet brinjals - ¼ kg.
Tamarind - Big gooseberry sized
(soaked)
Salt - according to taste
Oil - for frying
Mustard seeds - ¼ tsp.
Urad dhal - 1 tsp.

Method:

1. Cut brinjals into very fine pieces and soak it in water to prevent discolouring.

2. Strain the water and fry brinjals using enough oil.

3. Stir fry properly until raw flavour of brinjals are lost and transfer it to a plate.

4. In the remaining oil roast mustard, urad dhal and red chillies.

5. Allow all roasted ingredients to cool thoroughly and grind it together with salt and tamarind.

6. Add brinjals at the end and grind to a coarse paste.

7. Serve with idli, dosa, chappathi varieties.

Variation: Using the above method grind chutney using ridge gourd skin, instead of brinjals.

Note: This chutney tastes better if country brinjals are used. If it is not available hybrid brinjals can be used.

87. Ginger Chutney

Ingredients:

Ginger - 50 gms.
Red chillies - 5
Urad dhal - 2 tsps.
Bengal gram dhal - 1 Tbl.sp.
Grated fresh coconut - 2½ Tbl.sps.
Tamarind - Big gooseberry sized
      (soaked)
Salt - according to taste
Grated Jaggery - 1 Tbl.sp.
Oil - for frying, seasoning
Mustard seeds - ¼ tsp.

Method:

1. Scrape outer skin and cut ginger into round pieces.
2. Heat little oil in a kadai and fry red chillies, urad, bengal gram dhal until golden brown.
3. Fry ginger pieces separately in little oil.
4. Grind roasted, fried ingredients together with coconut, salt, tamarind, jaggery to coarse chutney consistency.
5. Heat one teaspoon of oil and add mustard seeds, allow to splutter and mix with chutney.

88. Ginger Sweet-Sour Chutney

Ingredients:

Grated fresh coconut - ¼ cup
Green chillies - 3
Ginger - 2 inch piece
      (scrape & then slice)
Tamarind - Big gooseberry sized
      (soaked & extracted)
Salt - to taste
Grated Jaggery - Little
Oil - 2 tsps.
Mustard seeds - ¼ tsp.
Asafoetida powder - 2 pinches
Curry leaves - 1 spring

Method:

1. Grind coconut, ginger, green chillies, salt, Jaggery along with thick tamarind extract, to chutney consistency.
2. Heat little oil in a 'kadai', add mustard, curry leaves and then asafoetida.
3. Add ground paste and stir for few minutes.
4. Take out, allow to cool and serve with pesarattu dosai or idli.

89. Ginger Spicy Chutney

Ingredients:

Ginger - 50 gms.
Green chillies - 4
Tamarind - Small lemon sized
Salt - to taste
Grated Jaggery - as desired
Finely cut coriander
         leaves - 1 Tbl.sp.
Oil - little
Mustard seeds - ¼ tsp.
Cumin seeds - ¼ tsp.
Dhania - ¼ tsp.
Fenugreek seeds - ¼ tsp.
Asafoetida powder - 2 pinches

Method:

1. Scrape outer skin and cut ginger into round, even sized pieces.

2. Cut chillies into round pieces.

3. Soak tamarind in hot water and squeeze thick extract. Strain and keep aside.

4. Grind ginger with chillies to a coarse paste in mixie.

5. Add salt, Jaggery, tamarind extract and grind to smooth paste.

6. Heat oil in a 'kadai' and add mustard seeds. Allow to splutter and then add dhania, cumin, fenugreek, asafoetida. Pour ground paste, allow to boil and remove from fire.

7. Mix finely cut coriander leaves to the chutney.

8. This chutney can be kept in refrigerator upto 15 days.

9. Serve with Idli, dosa, pongal or curd rice.

*Note: Ginger aids digesting process. Use it as often as possible in your diet.

90. Cabbage Chutney

Ingredients:

Big Onions - 3
Garlic - 5 flakes
Cabbage - ¼ kg.
Red chillies - 10
Fenugreek seeds - 2 tsps.
Mustard seeds - ½ tsp.
Thick tamarind extract -
                    2 Tbl.sps.
Salt - 1½ tsp. (approximate)
Grated jaggery - 1 Tbl.sp.
Asafoetida Powder - ¼ tsp.
Finely cut coriander leaves -
                    1 Tbl.sp.

Oil - for frying

Method:

1. Peel and chop onions, garlic.

2. Grate cabbage, fry in oil properly and keep aside.

3. Fry onions and garlic in oil separately until golden. Transfer to a plate and allow to cool.

4. Dry roast red chillies, fenugreek lightly and powder it along with salt.

5. Add fried onions, garlic, grated jaggery to that and grind to a coarse paste.

6. Mix tamarind extract, fried cabbage and finely cut coriander leaves with that.

7. Heat ½ tsp. of oil, add mustard seeds, allow to splutter, mix asafoetida powder and pour on top of chutney.

8. Mix well and serve this chutney with Idli, dosa, uttappam or chappathi.

Kothsu Varieties
91. Onion Kothsu

Ingredients:

Peeled small onions - ½ kg.
Tamarind - Small lemon sized
Salt - to taste
Coconut oil - optional (to taste)

Roast and grind:

Red Chillies - 8
Dhania - 2 tsps.
Grated fresh coconut - 1 cup

For seasoning:

Cumin seeds - ½ tsp.

Method:

1. Peel small onions and cut finely.
2. Soak tamarind in water and squeeze to a thick extract. Strain.
3. Heat little oil in a 'kadai' and roast chillies, dhania until crisp. Transfer to a plate and keep aside.
4. In that same kadai roast coconut until it turns dark brown in colour.
5. Grind chillies, dhania, coconut to a coarse chutney consistency.
6. Heat little oil, add cumin seeds, cut onions and fry until golden.
7. Pour tamarind extract, salt and boil.
8. Add ground paste and boil for few more minutes stirring in between.
9. Mix little coconut oil to chutney for taste and serve this with Idli, dosa, appam varieties.

   Variation: Omit tamarind. Grind few tomatoes along with other ingredients.

92. Green Chilli Kothsu

Ingredients:

Green chillies - 10
Big Onions - 2
Tamarind - Small lemon sized
Salt - 2 tsps.
Grated Jaggery - Little
Oil - for frying

For seasoning:

Mustard seeds, Urad dhal and
Asafoetida - Little

Method:

1. Cut onions and chillies into medium sized pieces.

2. Fry chillies in oil properly and transfer chillies alone in a plate.

3. In the same oil add seasonings and then cut onions.

4. Stir until onions are fried, add fried chillies also with that.

5. Allow to cool and grind to a coarse paste.

6. Add salt, jaggery, tamarind extract and boil until it turns thick.

7. Serve with pongal varieties.

   Beginner's Tip: Whenever frying green chillies cut it into 2 or 3 pieces. If whole green chillies are fried in oil it bursts which may splutter on your face.

93. Brinjal Kothsu

Ingredients:

Small Violet coloured
country brinjals - ¼ kg.
Green chillies - 4
(cut into round pieces)
Finely cut onion - ½ cup
Tamarind - Small lemon sized
(soaked & extracted)
Extracted Salt - to taste
Grated Jaggery / Sugar -
as desired
Turmeric powder - ¼ tsp.
Finely cut tomatoes - ¼ cup

Seasoning:

Mustard seeds - ¼ tsp.
Urad dhal - 1 tsp.
Bengal gram dhal - 1 tsp.
Asafoetida Powder - 2 pinches
Curry leaves - 1 spring

Method:

1. Cut brinjals into very fine pieces and keep immersed in water until required.

2. Heat oil in a 'kadai' and add chopped green chillies, brinjals.

3. Stir fry until brinjal turns into dark colour.

4. Pour tamarind extract add turmeric powder and boil until thick.

5. Switch off the stove and mash cooked brinjals properly using a masher.

6. Heat oil, add seasonings and then fry onions until golden.

7. Add tomatoes, stir until moisture evaporates and then add mashed brinjal, salt, sugar along with little water.

8. Cook until thick and serve along with hot pongal.

Variation:

Tomato kothsu: Omit brinjal in the above process. Blanch ¼ kg. tomatoes in hot water. Remove skin and mash. Reduce tamarind extract. Add little coconut extract at the end.

Ridge gourd kothsu: Scrape outer skin from ridge gourd, taste and select. (omit bitter ones) Cut finely and prepare kothsu as mentioned like brinjal kothsu.

94. Tomato Kothsu

Ingredients:

Ripe Tomatoes - ½ kg.
Salt - according to taste
Large Onions - 2 (cut finely)
Oil - for frying

Grind together:

Red chillies - 7
Dhania - 1 Tbl.sp.
Cumin seeds - 1½ tsp.
Grated fresh coconut - ¼ cup.
Bengal gram dhal - 2 tsps.

Method:

1. Heat water in a broad vessel.
2. When it starts boiling slip tomatoes in it one by one.
3. Allow to boil once and switch off the stove.
4. Allow to cool, strain water, remove outer skin and mash it well.
5. Heat oil in a 'kadai' add cut onions and fry until golden.
6. Add ground paste and stir until good aroma comes from the masala.
7. Add salt and mashed tomatoes.
8. Allow to boil for few minutes.
9. Serve with idli / pongal varieties.

Sweet Chutney Varieties
95. Coriander Sweet Chutney

Ingredients:

Coriander leaves - 1 big bunch
Scraped fresh ginger -
                    2 inch piece
Green chillies - 5
Tamarind - Lemon sized (soaked)
Grated Jaggery - 2 Tbl.sps.
Salt - according to taste
Oil - Little
Mustard seeds - ¼ tsp.

Method:

1. Pluck, wash and chop coriander leaves with its stem.
2. Add chopped ginger, chillies, salt, tamarind, jaggery to that and grind to a smooth paste.
3. Heat little oil, season mustard in it and add to chutney.
4. Serve with samosa, kachori varieties.

96. *Tomato Sweet Chutney*

Ingredients:

Firm ripe sweet Tomatoes - ½ kg.
Sugar - 200 gms.
Salt - 1 tsp.
White Vinegar - 2 Tbl.sps.

Pound Coarsely:

Peeled small onions - 3
Scraped ginger - 1 inch piece
Garlic - 2 flakes
Red chillies - 5
Cardamoms - 2
Cinnamon - 1 inch piece
Pound above ingredients coarsely
and tie it in a piece of muslin cloth.

Method:

1. Heat water in a broad vessel.

2. When it starts boiling add washed tomatoes, allow to boil once and remove from fire.

3. Close with a lid and keep aside for few minutes.

4. Strain the water, remove outer skin of tomatoes and mash it. Strain through large eyed strainer.

5. To the strained tomato puree add spice bag, salt, sugar and boil steadily in medium flame. (to be continued)

6. Stir in between and boil steadily until it reaches sauce consistency.

7. Switch off the stove, discard masala bag add vinegar, allow to cool and bottle it.

8. This chutney can be kept for few months. Serve with all deep fried items.

   Note: According to the sweetness of tomatoes quantity of sugar, vinegar can be adjusted.

97. Apple Sweet Chutney

Ingredients:

Small cooking apples - ¼ kg.
Lemon Juice - 1 Tbl.sp.
Large onion - 1
Scraped ginger - 1 inch piece
Peeled garlic - 2 flakes
Red chilli powder - 1 tsp.
Salt - according to taste
Vinegar - 2 Tbl.sps.
Sugar - 1½ tsp.
Roasted Jeera powder - 2 tsps.

Method:

1. Wash, Scrape outer skin and grate apples.
2. Mix lemon juice with that to prevent discolouration.
3. Peel and dice onion.
4. Grate ginger using fine cheese grater.
5. Take onion, garlic, ginger in a vessel. Pour just enough water to cover it.
6. Cook it in medium flame until onion becomes soft.
7. Mash well, add grated apples and pour little more water to cover it.
8. Heat it in medium flame stirring in between until the mixture turns thick.
9. Add salt, chilli powder, sugar, vinegar and mix well.
10. Switch off the stove and add roasted cumin powder. Mix well, allow to cool and bottle it.
11. This chutney can be kept in refrigerator for more than a month.
12. Serve as sandwich spread. Children like it along with Idli, dosa, chappathi varieties also.

Note: 1. Onions should be cooked droperly. Then only it can be mashed well. Otherwise allow to cool and grind it coarsely in a mixie. 2. Use only small, sour apples for this chutney for better taste.

98. Date Chutney (For Pani puri)

Ingredients:

Seedless dates - 10 pieces
Kismis - 1 Tbl.sp.
Tamarind - Lemon sized
Grated Jaggery - ¼ cup
Salt - ½ tsp.
Red chilli powder - ½ tsp.
Roasted, powdered
      cumin seeds - ½ tsp.

Method:

1. Soak dates, kismis, tamarind in just enough water to cover it, for ½ hour.

2. Grind it in a mixie, add salt, chilli powder, jaggery and grind again to smooth paste.

3. Strain it through a tamarind strainer.

4. Wash the mixie, pour through the strainer, so that ground paste can be strained properly.

5. Heat the chutney in a thick vessel, stirring in between until it turns shiny.

6. Add roasted cumin powder, mix well, allow to cool and store it in a container.

7. This can be kept in refrigerator for a month also.

8. Use this for pani puri, bhel puri, samosa, kachorie and chat varieties.

99. Date Sweet - Sour Chutney

Ingredients:

Seedless soft dates - 50 gms
Red chillies - 2
White Vinergar - 2 Tbl.sps.
Sugar - 2 Tbl.sps.
Salf - according to taste
Garlic - 3 flakes
Ginger - 1 inch piece

Method:

1. Chop dates and soak it in just enough water for 15 minutes.
2. Cook it in medium flame until dates become soft.
3. Mash it using a wooden masher.
4. Break red chillies, remove seeds and soak in vinegar for 10 minutes.
5. Add ginger, garlic, sugar, salt to the soaked chillies and grind to a paste.
6. Dilute it and boil for few minutes.
7. Add mashed dates at the end, cook for a minute and remove from fire.
8. Serve along with deep fried dishes like samosa, bonda, vadai etc.,

100. Dry Fruit Sweet & Spicy Chutney

Ingredients:

Tamarind - Lemon sized
Grated Jaggery - 2 Tbl.sps.
Kismis - 1 Tbl.sp.
Roasted Cashews - 10
Roasted Peanuts - 1 Tbl.sp.
Grated dry coconut - 1 Tbl.sp.
Sesame seeds - 1 tsp.
Salt - to taste
Roasted, powdered
          cumin seeds - ½ tsp.
Red chilli powder - ½ tsp.

Method:

1. Soak tamarind in enough water, squeeze and prepare extract for ᴸ cup.
2. Dry roast seasame seeds, grated dry coconut (kopra) separately until brown.
3. Add roasted peanuts, cashews along with that and powder it in a small mixie. (Run mixie at low speed at short intervals to powder it)
4. Mix salt, Jaggery, chilli powder, kismis with diluted tamarind extract and boil until it gets a shine.
5. Switch off the stove, add cumin powder and mix well.
6. As this is very tasty and nutritions, children love to eat it with bread, Idli, dosa varieties.

OUR BOOKS ARE SOLD AT :

At BANGALORE:
VASAN BOOK DEPOT
25,Vasan Towers, Goods shed
Road, Bangalore:53

T.N.KRISHNIAH SETTY & SON
234, Chickpet,Bangalore:53

GANGARAMS
72. M.G.Road, Bangalore: 1

SAPNA BOOK HOUSE
(Opp: Tribhuvan theatre)
Gandhi nagar. Bangalore:9.

HIGGINBOTHAMS LTD
68, M.G.Road, Bangalore:1.

A.S.BOOK DISTRIBUTORS
1,Sanjeeva niack Lane,
Avenue Road Cross
Bangalore:2

PRISM - THE BOOK SHOP
16, 11th Main, 4th Block
Jaya Nagar, Banglore:11

VINAYAKA BOOK
Distributors
49,St Johns Road,
Bangalore:42

Land Mark - Koramangala

AT MYSORE:
Geetha Book House
K.R.Circle, Mysore:1

At VILLIPURAM
SRI KANNIKA
PARAMESWARI STORE
91, Kamarajar street.

AT PONDICHERY:
Higginbothams Ltd
34,Ambour Salai,Pondichery.

SRI VIJAYAGANAPATHI
STORES
109,Easwaran koil st,Pondy:1

AT ERODE:
Sri Kannan Dept Stores
49.27, Periyar street, Erode:1

AT TRICHY:

AGASTHIAR BOOK DEPOT
9A,Clives Bldg,Nandhi koil st
Trichy:2

VISVAS BOOK CENRE
Clives BuildingTheppakulam

Femina Shop

Mangal & Mangal

At HOSUR:
Coimbatore North Sarvodaya
77 E, Indra Nagar, Bagalur
Road, Hosur:9

INDIAN BOOK CENTRE
11/7, Ramar koil st.

AT SALEM:
S.BANGARU CHETTY
17, Fort Main Road. Salem:2
Phone:4031540

CHANDRA BOOK SHOP
No.5, Car Street.

SAI GIRIDHAR STORES
Opp:Sarada College,Fair lands.

BHARATHI SUPER
MARKET- Hasthampatti.

Nilgiris - Salem

At NAMAKKAL:
Namakkal Super Market'
9, Thuraiyur Road.

AT KARUR:
SRI VANI BOOK SHOP
CNKK Complex,
 176-A,Jawahar bazar,Karur-1

Thaila Silks
200, Jawahar Bazar, Karur

AT COIMBATORE:
CHERAN BOOK HOUSE
137,Big Bazaar Street,
Coimbatore-1

S S BOOK HOUSE
Lakshmi Complex,
Cross cut Rd,Gandhipuram.

VIJAYA PATHIPPAKAM
20, Raja street, Coimbatore:1

Kannan Dept Stores
130, Rajaji st, Coimbatore:9

Vinupriya Home Foods
D B Road, R S Puram,
Coimbatore : 2

Read N Reach
490, DB Road, R S Puram

AT KRISHNAGIRI:
Mrs.C.BARATHI
D-14, 2nd Cross,
Co-op Colony Road.

AT MADURAI:
MALLIGAI BOOK CENTRE
Opp : Railway station,
Madurai : 1

MEENAKSHI BOOK SHOP
Shivalingam Towers
99-B East Avani Mula st,
Madurai:1

New Century Book House
80,West Tower Street
Madurai : 1

At TUTICORIN
SUMANGALI SUPER MARKET
239, North Car St, Tuticorin:2

EAGLE BOOK CENTRE
1A/25, Palayamkottai Road
Tuticorin

AT Dindigul :
AYYANAR BOOK CENTRE
14, Dudley School Building
Dindigul

At Tirunelveli:
EAGLE BOOK CENTRE
169, Trivendrum Road,
Palayamkottai.

AT RAJAPALAYAM:
UMA CHITRA AGENCIES
52/ 16-a, THMBAPILLAI ST
RAJAPALAYAM : 117

At Krishnagiri
Sri Sarathi Home Neds
229/b, Chennai Salai
Krishnagiri:1

At BOMBAY:
GIRI TRADING AGENCY
Opp: Post Office, Matunga,
Bombay: 19

Reliance Liesure - Stores
RelianceTime Out Stores
COCHIN, BANGALORE,
HYDERABAD,JAIPUR
Mysore

At Udumalaipet:
Udumalai Book Centre
2, Sreenivasa Street

<u>Note:</u> Please Send Demand drft in Advance with extra charge of Rs.30/- for each order of maximum
4 books. We will send Books by COURIER

OUR BOOKS ARE SOLD IN CHENNAI AT :

PRADEEP ENTERPRISES, 20,Poes Garden,Chennai:86.

HIGGINBOTHAMS LTD
814,Anna Salai. Chennai:2.

KARTHIK BOOK SHOP
30,South Mada st
Mylapore, Chennai: 4

VIJAYA STORES
24/1,South Mada Street,
Mylapore. Chennai: 4.

Giri Trading Co
10,Kapaleswarar Sannidhi
Mylapore.

Cross Word
82, TTK Road, Alwarpet

Nilgiris -Chetpet
879, P.H Road (Next to
Ega)

NEW BOOK LAND
52,North Usman Road,
T.Nagar

MADRAS BOOK HOUSE
4,Ranganathan st, T.Nagar

ODYSSEY
15, First Main Road,
Gandhinagar, Adyar.

Nilgiris
Annai Velankani Church Rd
Besant Nagar.

WORDS & WORTHS
26,Second Avenue,
Besant Nagar

CONNEXIONS
W-122,3rd Avenue,
Annanagar
Velachery, Mahindra City,
Saligramam.

Nilgiris
2nd Avenue, Anna Nagar.

YESESS SUPER MARKET
T-101, Anna Nagar

Murugan Stores
1035, E V High Road,
Arumbakam

C L S Book Shop
68, Evening Bazar,
Chennai : 3

BOOK PALACE
12, Pycrofts Road,
Triplicane.

SUDHA STORES
54,Big Street, Triplicane.

M.K.STORES
40, Bunder st,
Chennai:1

Nilgiris
321,Arcot Road, Doshi Garden
Vadapalani

CONNEXIONS
48,Arcot Road
Saligramam, Chennai.

PANDIAN SUPER MARKET
82, Arcot Road
Virugambakkam

PONNU SUPER MARKET
Near Rathi Theatre
Ambattur

LAND MARK
Nungambakam High Road,
SPENCERS,Citi Centre, Dr
R.K. Road, AMPA MALL.

**RHYTHAM BOOK
DISTRIBUTORS**
93, Jeenis road, Saidapet

**LEO BOOK
DISTRIBUTORS**
1st Main Road, CI T Nagar

Nilgiris
13/A, Main Road, Velachery

JEEVAN SUPER MARKET
52, 10th Avenue
Ashok Nagar

**SRI VENKATESWARA
SUPER MARKET, 28,11th
Main Rd,**
Vijayanagar, Velachery,
Chennai:42

**KIRAN BOOK
DISTRIBUTIRS**
16, State Bank Street,
Chennai: 600 002

ANGELS
AC-15,Second Avenue,
Anna Nagar.

ANGELS
38/1, 100 ft bye pass Road
Velachery. CH:42

**FORWARD MARKETING
AGENCY,**
41, Anderson 1st Street,
Chennai: 1

Easwar Books
27, Natesan Road
T.Nagar, Chennai:17

Jeevan Super Market
Mugappair

SRIRAM & Co
32, M R M Road
Tambaram

Nilgiris - Tambaram
110,VGP Srinivasa Nagar
Madambakam Mian Road
Rajakilipakkam
Chennai:73

Nilgiris - Porur
96, Trunk Road
Porur, Ch: 116

Santhosh Super Market
815, MTH Road, Ch:50

Nilgiris - Valasarvakam
72, Arcot Road
Valasarvakam

Kamakshi Amman Koil
Mangaadu
Chennai

At Kanchipuram:
Guru Book Centre
16, Nellu kaara st

Sabari Book House
Nilgiris
42, CP RAmaswamy Road
Chennai: 18

For Trade Enquiries contact:
PRADEEP ENTERPRISES
20/90, POES GARDEN,
CHENNAI : 600086

<u>Note:</u> Please Send Demand Draft in Advance with extra charge of Rs.30/- for each order of
maximum 4 books. We will send Books by COURIER